DOING YOUR BEST

*A 4-week course to help junior highers
discover God's views on striving for the best in life*

by Michelle Anthony

Group®
Loveland, Colorado

Group®

Doing Your Best
Copyright © 1993 Group Publishing, Inc.

Credits
Edited by Amy Nappa
Cover designed by Diane Whisner
Illustrations by Raymond Medici
Cover photo by Brenda Rundback and David Priest

ISBN 1-55945-142-4
12 11 10 9 8 7 6   04 03 02 01 00 99 98
Printed in the United States of America.

CONTENTS

DOING YOUR BEST

Sara is confused. At church her parents are well-known and even lead a Bible study. Yet at home her father is verbally abusive, constantly putting Sara and her mother down.

Mark is confused. His teacher recently made a big speech to the class about not cheating, but a few days later she was arrested for falsifying school documents.

"Doing Your Best" Enters Many Arenas

- Sixty-nine percent of junior highers value having fun in life compared to 66 percent who want God to be at the center of their lives.

- About 62 percent of students feel strong friendships are extremely important.

- While 43 percent of teenagers believe deep religious faith is very important, 44 percent think that having lots of money is just as important.

- Only 25 percent of students say they take their homework seriously, putting in 6 hours or more a week.

No wonder teenagers don't understand what it means to do their best; their examples are failing miserably. The messages society is sending conflict with the values of the Bible.

While you're urging students to avoid sexual activity, the media use sex to sell absolutely everything. We say truthfulness and integrity are important, but those who cheat often prosper. Parents who push their children to get good grades may be too busy to help with homework. It's also not uncommon for "religious" kids to have no idea what it means to live like a Christian.

This course helps junior highers understand what God has in mind for the lives of Christians. They will discover God's views on striving for their best in areas such as their relationships with God and others, their school lives and their value systems. Students will have the opportunity to hear God's personal message on how to live to their potential even when others don't.

By the end of this course, your students will
- experience the importance of staying in a close relationship with God,
- discover ways to build and maintain strong relationships,
- learn how doing their best in school is a reflection of God to others and
- explore how their values compare to God's values.

COURSE OBJECTIVES

HOW TO USE THIS COURSE

ACTIVE
LEARNING

Think back on an important lesson you've learned in life. Did you learn it from reading about it? from hearing about it? from something you experienced? Chances are, the most important lessons you've learned came from something you experienced. That's what active learning is—learning by doing. And active learning is a key element in Group's Active Bible Curriculum®.

Active learning leads students in doing things that help them understand important principles, messages and ideas. It's a discovery process that helps kids internalize what they learn.

Each lesson section in Group's Active Bible Curriculum plays an important part in active learning:

The Opener involves kids in the topic in fun and unusual ways.

The Action and Reflection includes an experience designed to evoke specific feelings in the students. This section also processes those feelings through "How did you feel?" questions and applies the message to situations kids face.

The Bible Application actively connects the topic with the Bible. It helps kids see how the Bible is relevant to the situations they face.

The Commitment helps students internalize the Bible's message and commit to making changes in their lives.

The Closing funnels the lesson's message into a time of creative reflection and prayer.

When you put all the sections together, you get a lesson that's fun to teach. And kids get messages they'll remember.

BEFORE THE 4-WEEK SESSION

● Read the Introduction, the Course Objectives and This Course at a Glance.

● Decide how you'll publicize the course using the clip art on the Publicity Page (p. 9). Prepare fliers, newsletter articles and posters as needed.

● Look at the Bonus Ideas (p. 43) and decide which ones you'll use.

• Read the opening statements, Objectives and Bible Basis for the lesson. The Bible Basis shows how specific passages relate to junior highers and middle schoolers today.

• Choose which Opener and Closing options to use. Each is appropriate for a different kind of group.

• Gather necessary supplies from This Lesson at a Glance.

• Read each section of the lesson. Adjust where necessary for your class size and meeting room.

• The approximate minutes listed give you an idea of how long each activity will take. Each lesson is designed to take 35 to 60 minutes. Shorten or lengthen activities as needed to fit your group.

• If you see you're going to have extra time, do an activity or two from the "If You Still Have Time . . ." box or from the Bonus Ideas (p. 43).

• Dive into the activities with the kids. Don't be a spectator. The lesson will be more successful and rewarding to both you and your students.

• Though some kids may at first think certain activities are "silly," they'll enjoy them, and they'll remember the messages from these activities long after the lesson is over. As one Active Bible Curriculum user has said, "I can ask the kids questions about a lesson I did three weeks ago, and they actually remember what I taught!" And that's the whole idea of teaching . . . isn't it?

Have fun with the activities you lead. Remember, it is Jesus who encourages us to become "like little children." Besides, how often do your kids get *permission* to express their childlike qualities?

• The answers given after discussion questions are responses your students *might* give. They aren't the only answers or the "right" answers. If needed, use them to spark discussion. Kids won't always say what you wish they'd say. That's why some of the responses given are negative or controversial. If someone responds negatively, don't be shocked. Accept the person and use the opportunity to explore other angles of the issue.

THIS COURSE AT A GLANCE

Before you dive into the lessons, familiarize yourself with each lesson aim. Then read the scripture passages.
- Study them as a background to the lessons.
- Use them as a basis for your personal devotions.
- Think about how they relate to kids' circumstances today.

LESSON 1: WHO'S NUMBER ONE?

Lesson Aim: To help junior highers explore how to have an excellent relationship with God.

Bible Basis: Joshua 1:8; Matthew 14:23; and James 1:27.

LESSON 2: FIRST-RATE FRIENDSHIPS

Lesson Aim: To help junior highers explore the components of building and maintaining positive relationships.

Bible Basis: John 13:34-35; Romans 12:14-18; and Ephesians 4:29-32.

LESSON 3: BE TRUE TO YOUR SCHOOL

Lesson Aim: To challenge junior highers to make their school lives a reflection of their spiritual lives.

Bible Basis: 2 Timothy 2:1-7.

LESSON 4: CHOOSING OR LOSING GOD'S VALUES

Lesson Aim: To help junior highers choose values according to God's Word.

Bible Basis: 1 Samuel 16:1-13.

PUBLICITY PAGE

Grab your junior highers' attention! Photocopy this page, and then cut out and paste the clip art of your choice in your church bulletin or newsletter to advertise this course on doing your best. Or photocopy and use the ready-made flier as a bulletin insert. Permission to photocopy this clip art is granted for local church use.

Splash the clip art on posters, fliers or even postcards! Just add the vital details: the date and time the course begins and where you'll meet.

It's that simple.

DOING YOUR BEST

DOING YOUR BEST

Doing Your BEST

A 4-week course to help junior highers discover God's views on striving for the best in life.

Go Team! Go Team! Go Team!

Come to

On

At

Come learn what it means to do your best!

WHO'S NUMBER ONE?

"A relationship with God? I thought Christians just had to go to church a lot."

Many junior highers have been going to church for years yet still find it difficult to fully express what it means to be a Christian. This lesson will help your students explore what it means to have a dynamic and personal relationship with God.

To help junior highers explore how to have an excellent relationship with God.

LESSON AIM

Students will
- **experience the importance of staying close to God,**
- **determine what is needed for spiritual survival,**
- **discover the importance of support and accountability and**
- **examine their commitment to God.**

OBJECTIVES

Look up the following scriptures. Then read the background paragraphs to see how the passages relate to your junior highers and middle schoolers.

In **Joshua 1:8,** God tells Joshua how to succeed as he takes on the responsibility of leading Israel.

With encouragement and admonishment, God urges Joshua to intently meditate on his Word. God promises that this will bring success for Joshua.

Though junior highers don't live in Joshua's time, it's just as crucial for them to study and live by God's Word. This is a priceless tool for living a strong Christian life in a non-Christian world. God still delivers success and prosperity to those who follow him like Joshua did.

BIBLE BASIS
JOSHUA 1:8
MATTHEW 14:23
JAMES 1:27

Matthew 14:23 gives an example of the importance of prayer.

Jesus was followed by crowds wherever he went yet longed for time alone with his Father. Determined to have privacy, he met the needs of the people and still made time to go to a mountain for prayer.

If Jesus found it beneficial to pray, we should as well. Prayer can make a seemingly intangible God real to students. Demonstrating the importance of prayer will open the door for kids to have a dynamic and personal relationship with God.

James 1:27 tells what it means to live like a Christian.

James names two ways a Christian demonstrates that his or her faith is true. The first is caring for those in need and the second is keeping away from the world's bad influences. Junior highers may claim to be Christians yet fail to understand the lifestyle James discusses. They may think church attendance is all that's expected of them as Christians. They need instruction regarding the biblical lifestyle, as well as a model to follow.

THIS LESSON AT A GLANCE

Section	Minutes	What Students Will Do	Supplies
Opener (Option 1)	5 to 10	**Come Closer**—Participate in a perception game.	Masking tape, two pairs of binoculars
(Option 2)		**I'm Stuck on You**—Participate in a close-contact activity of skill.	Small candies, coins, jumpropes, masking tape, taffy
Action and Reflection	15 to 20	**Survival Strategy**—Choose supplies for surviving a plane crash.	"Survival Strategy" handouts (p. 18), color markers, pencils
Bible Application	10 to 15	**Staying Alive**—Create skits based on scripture references.	Bibles, chalkboard, chalk
Commitment	5 to 10	**He Ain't Heavy, He's My Brother**—Complete a relay of creativity and support.	"Survival Strategy" handouts from "Survival Strategy" activity
Closing (Option 1)	up to 5	**Chicken?**—Compare the commitment of two animals.	Bacon, an egg
(Option 2)		**Common Denominator**—Determine what a variety of objects have in common.	Box of items representing commitment

The Lesson

☐ OPTION 1: COME CLOSER

Tape to the floor two pieces of masking tape approximately 6 feet long and parallel to each other. Form two teams and give each team a pair of binoculars.

Say: **When I say "go," each person on your team must walk along the piece of tape without falling off. The only catch is that you must walk while looking through the wrong end of the binoculars. The first team done wins. Ready? Go!**

When teams are finished, ask:

● **Why was it difficult to walk across the tape?** (It was hard to see it; it was too far away; I couldn't keep my balance.)

● **How is this game like our relationship with God?** (God seems far away at times; it's hard to walk with God when he's so far away; I can't see God clearly.)

Say: **Sometimes it seems that God is far away even though he's not, just like the line seemed far away even though it was close. Today we're going to look at why it's important to stay close to God.**

☐ OPTION 2: I'M STUCK ON YOU

Have students form pairs. Give each pair the following items: six pieces of small candy, six coins and a jump-rope. Instruct them to place all items on the floor. Tape each pair together as they stand back to back. (Wrap the masking tape around their waists two or three times.)

Say: **Without breaking your tape, you must accomplish the following tasks: Feed your partner three pieces of candy, pick up three coins off the floor, jump rope as a pair three times and touch three things not on your body starting with the letter "d." The first pair to finish and sit down wins. If your tape breaks, you're disqualified. Ready? Go!**

Play until there's a winner. For fun, give out taffy or another "sticky" candy to winners. Ask:

● **How did it feel to be stuck to someone? Explain.** (Frustrating because it was hard to move; tricky because we had to work together.)

● **What was difficult about this game?** (I was afraid to break the tape; I had to wait for my partner.)

● **Why do you think the winners won?** (They stuck closest to each other; they followed each other's moves.)

● **How are these strategies for winning like strategies for improving our relationship with God?** (The closer we are to God, the better we know what he wants; staying close to God helps us "win" in life.)

Say: **Sticking close to God makes us winners in real life, too. Today we're going to look at why it's important to stay close to God and how to do it.**

SURVIVAL STRATEGY

Before the meeting, photocopy the "Survival Strategy" handouts (p. 18) and make a red, blue, green or brown X at the top of each one. Mark the same amount with each color and mix the handouts up to be distributed randomly.

Give students each a pencil and a handout, and instruct them to keep the handout face down. Tell them it represents a passport to one of four places in the world: the Amazon Jungle, the Pacific Ocean, the Swiss Alps or the Sahara Desert.

Say: **Imagine that each of you has taken a vacation by plane to a certain destination. Ironically all four planes have crashed. You have ten minutes to locate your fellow passengers and choose the five most important items from the supply list needed for survival in your region. Find people with matching X's on their passports and complete your handout with them. Ready? Go!**

After ten minutes, have groups come together and report what supplies they chose and why. Then ask:

● **What was it like being able to choose only five things for survival?** (Impossible; I was anxious; challenging.)

● **Why was it important to know where you crashed?** (You have different needs in different places; so we could set our priorities.)

● **How did you decide what things to choose?** (We thought ahead to what we might face; we thought of someone who had really crashed.)

● **How is this game like our relationship with God?** (We have to be prepared in the world; we need God to survive; we have to think ahead to what might happen in a certain situation.)

● **What do you need to "survive" being a Christian?** (A Bible; strong Christian friends; time with God.)

Say: **When you became a Christian, it wasn't by some strange accident. You decided that a relationship with God was important to you. To keep this relationship from becoming a disaster and instead, to make it the best, you need certain things to survive or to keep you alive spiritually. Let's learn more about keeping our relationship with God flying high!**

ACTION AND REFLECTION
(15 to 20 minutes)

STAYING ALIVE

Form three groups and assign each group one of the following verses: Joshua 1:8; Matthew 14:23; and James 1:27. Give each group five minutes and 12 seconds to look up the verse, decide how the verse relates to a healthy relationship with God and come up with a two-part skit.

The first part of the skit should demonstrate how *not* obeying the verse affects a person's relationship with God. The second part should show how obeying the verse improves a person's relationship with God and shows others what being a Christian really means. For example, the first part could portray a student who claims to be a Christian but ignores the need of a friend who forgot his lunch money. The second part could portray this student sharing his lunch and telling his friend how God motivated him to help.

After each group has performed, have the other groups guess what they were trying to portray. Write the qualities on the chalkboard and ask:

● **How did you feel doing or watching the first part of each skit? Explain.** (Guilty because I do the same things; glad because I know a lot of our group members try hard to live this way.)

● **How are the characters in your skit like people today?** (Some give others a bad impression of Christians; some think being a Christian means just going to church.)

● **From what we have seen through reading our Bibles and watching these skits, how would you summarize God's plan for a strong relationship with him?** (We need to read our Bibles; caring for others is important; prayer is a way to share our lives with God.)

● **Why is it sometimes hard to do these things even though we know they keep us close to God?** (We don't make time; we forget; our friends pull us away from God.)

Say: **God wants to have an excellent relationship with each person here, but it takes effort and commitment on our part. We've just learned what we need to do. Now let's see how we can help each other do these things.**

HE AIN'T HEAVY, HE'S MY BROTHER

Form teams of no more than five students. Put one chair per team on the opposite side of the room.

Say: **Each team must together run around the chair five times. However, each lap you must carry a different member of your team in a different way (on your shoulders, on your back, and so on). The first team to finish wins.**

Afterward ask:

● **How did you feel when you were carried?** (I felt important; I was afraid they would drop me.)

● **What was the most difficult part of this game?** (Trying to think of new ways to carry someone; it was hard to carry them because they were heavier than I thought.)

● **How is this game like our relationships with other Christians?** (Sometimes others need a lot of support and it's like carrying them; everyone has different needs, like everyone had to be carried differently.)

● **How can you support others in their relationship with God?** (Pray for them; read the Bible together; encourage them with a note.)

Have team members stay in their groups and refer to the "Supplies" list on the "Survival Strategy" handouts. Instruct students to work together to choose a different item to represent each person in their group. Tell kids to explain how that item demonstrates being supportive. For example, "Bob, you're like a life raft because you're always pulling people out of trouble" or "Liz, you're like a candy bar because you cheer people on and give them more energy."

Say: **Having a great relationship with God isn't always easy. By supporting one another we can help other Christians stay close to God.**

Table Talk

The Table Talk activity in this course helps junior highers and middle schoolers discuss with their parents a Christian perspective on persevering and succeeding in relationships.

If you choose to use the Table Talk activity, this is a good time to show students the "Table Talk" handout (p. 19). Ask them to spend time with their parents completing it.

Before kids leave, give them each the "Table Talk" handout to take home, or tell them you'll be sending it to their parents. Tell kids to be prepared to report next week on their experiences with the handout.

Or use the Table Talk idea found in the Bonus Ideas (p. 44) for a meeting based on the handout.

CLOSING
(up to 5 minutes)

☐ OPTION 1: CHICKEN?

Say: **No matter how much others encourage you, you're the one who has to decide how committed you are to God. There are many levels of commitment. Let's look at a couple.**

Hold up a package of bacon and an egg, and ask:

● **Which represents a higher level of commitment? Explain.** (The bacon because the pig gave its life, but the chicken just gave an egg.)

Say: **Ask yourself right now if you are a chicken or a pig. Are you giving a little, or are you giving all of your life to God?**

Ask:

● **What would it take for us to be a bunch of "pigs" for God?** (We'd have to spend more time with God; we might have to change some of our habits.)

Say: **Having a great relationship with God involves spending time reading the Bible, praying and caring for others. Making a commitment to do these things is the most important commitment you'll ever make.**

Say a closing prayer for your class. Then have kids stand up and do their best pig imitations after you say "amen."

☐ OPTION 2: COMMON DENOMINATOR

Put together a box full of items that represent the idea of commitment. Examples are a wedding ring, a football jersey, a campaign button or bumper sticker, a cross, a picture of your class and an IOU. Pull out items one at a time and have people try to guess what they have in common.

Say: **These items have one thing in common: They represent a personal commitment. There are many things we can commit ourselves to, but none is as important as God.**

Have students each find a partner and share a way they need to be more committed in their relationship with God. Close by having the kids pray for their partners.

If You Still Have Time . . .

Me and God—Form groups of no more than four and have each group develop a creative time with God. This time should include prayer, Bible reading and caring for others, as described in the lesson. Allow each group to present its plan and then have all groups vote on which is the most creative. Discuss other ways kids can improve their time with God.

Doing Your Best—Have students brainstorm situations where they have the opportunity to choose to do their best for God or not. (For example, the teacher didn't mark a wrong answer on an exam.) After each situation is mentioned, ask:
- What is the easiest thing to do?
- What is the best thing to do and why?

SURVIVAL STRATEGY

Your plane has crashed. Please check your passport and use this color code to find out where you've crashed: red=the Amazon Jungle, blue=the Pacific Ocean, green=the Swiss Alps and brown=the Sahara Desert.

After you locate your fellow passengers, look over the supply list and choose the five most important things you will need to survive in your region.

SUPPLIES:

- waterproof matches,
- a tarp,
- six sleeping bags,
- a compass,
- three jugs of water,
- a battery-operated fan,
- four candy bars,
- lipstick,
- shark repellent,
- a lantern,
- an empty ice chest,
- a life raft,
- snowshoes,
- a Walkman,
- SPF 30 sunscreen,
- a kerosene lamp,
- dehydrated food packs,
- rope,
- two small jackets,
- an umbrella,
- a navigation map,
- a clock,
- a razor blade,
- an inner tube,
- seven flares,
- an old boat motor
- and a radio.

Table Talk

To the Parent: We're involved in a junior high course at church called *Doing Your Best*. Students are exploring what it means to do their best in various areas of life. We'd like you and your teenager to discuss this important topic. Use this "Table Talk" page to help you do that.

Parent

Complete the following sentences:
- The best part of being in a relationship with God is...
- One thing I wish I'd tried harder at in school was...
- I appreciate my friends who have...
- The most valuable quality one can have is...

Junior higher

Complete the following sentences:
- I want to know God better because...
- The area of school I want to do my best in is...
- I could be a better friend to others by...
- One thing I value in life is...

Parent and junior higher

Tell whether you think the statements below are true or false and why.
- God doesn't have time to worry if I tell a white lie or not, since he's concerned about the big picture.
- God likes me better when I'm being good.
- A good personal relationship with Jesus requires as much time as my relationship with my best friend.
- I will be happier if I obey God and his Word even when the decision is hard.

Read Colossians 3:17 aloud together and discuss these questions:
- What is an example of a word that would be glorifying to God?
- What is an example of a deed that would be glorifying to God?

Pray together that God will enable you to excel in your relationship with him and to not settle for mediocrity.

FIRST-RATE FRIENDSHIPS

"If I like my friends so much, why do we fight all the time?"

The world of a junior higher seems to revolve around his or her friends. Yet many young teenagers are unsure of how to build strong relationships. Trivial misunderstandings become causes of major fights, and soon the friendships are over.

This lesson will help students discover how to strive for the best in their relationships in order to build strong and lasting friendships.

LESSON AIM

To help junior highers explore the components of building and maintaining positive relationships.

OBJECTIVES

Students will
- discover the difference between productive and destructive qualities in relationships,
- witness the importance of communication in healthy relationships,
- explore scriptural guidelines for interpersonal relationships and
- discover qualities that make them good friends.

BIBLE BASIS

JOHN 13:34-35
ROMANS 12:14-18
EPHESIANS 4:29-32

Look up the following scriptures. Then read the background paragraphs to see how the passages relate to your junior highers and middle schoolers.

In John 13:34-35, Christ tells us to love one another.

God's love toward all people is the example for us to follow. Jesus says the world will know we belong to God by our love for one another.

While the thought of telling others about Jesus strikes fear in the heart of many teenagers, this command leads to a simple way of sharing God's message. Students can express their belief in God to their friends through their actions of love.

Romans 12:14-18 gives further instructions for relationships.

These verses describe how to act toward friends and enemies. We are instructed to choose for friends people who seem "unimportant" and to live in peace with others.

Junior highers often see relationships as ways to gain popularity or security. And when teenagers are wronged, getting even is important for maintaining dignity. This passage expresses God's desire for us to be at peace with all people, whether we like them or not.

Ephesians 4:29-32 gives specific directions for the treatment of others.

These verses instruct us to speak only those words which will build up others. We should not speak harsh and hurtful words. Finally, Christians should express kindness, love and forgiveness to others.

The qualities listed in these verses don't seem to be those of highest importance to most junior highers. However, the passage closes with the words "just as God forgave you in Christ." If God can treat us with love and forgiveness, we can certainly learn to express these qualities to others.

THIS LESSON AT A GLANCE

Section	Minutes	What Students Will Do	Supplies
Opener (Option 1)	5 to 10	**Buddy Blues**—Brainstorm things they don't want a friend to do.	Chalkboard, chalk
(Option 2)		**Order in the Court**—Act as a jury in three cases.	
Action and Reflection	10 to 15	**I Can't Hear You**—Participate in a loud and crazy communication game.	Bibles, paper, pencils, radio
Bible Application	15 to 20	**Mission Impossible**—Engage in a spy maneuver to locate good qualities from the Bible.	Paper, pencils, scissors, "Mission Impossible" handouts (p. 28), chalkboard, chalk, Bibles
Commitment	5 to 10	**It's Written All Over Your Face**—Discover good qualities in their own lives by getting clues from others.	Pencils, masking tape
Closing (Option 1)	up to 5	**Relate-o-Meter**—Rate themselves as to how good of a friend they are.	Masking tape, marker
(Option 2)		**Center of God's Love**—See the difference God's love makes.	

The Lesson

☐ OPTION 1: BUDDY BLUES

Number from one to 10 on the chalkboard. Have students call out the 10 worst things a friend can do to them. Write items on the chalkboard as they're mentioned and then allow students to debate to narrow down the list if there are more than 10 items.

When the list is complete, ask:

● **How do you respond when someone you consider a friend does one of these things to you?** (I get angry; I feel cheated.)

● **Are you able to continue your friendship with a person who treats you like this? Why or why not?** Answers will vary.

Say: **Doing the things on this list will probably lead to problems in your relationships. Today we're going to talk about doing our best in building and maintaining relationships. Now that we've determined how we *shouldn't* treat one another, let's see how we *should* act toward others.**

☐ OPTION 2: ORDER IN THE COURT

Say: **Imagine that this class is now a court of law, and you are the jury. I'll read three situations and after each one you'll vote on what you think each person should do in his or her situation.**

Read the following "cases" and after each one have the jury vote on its favorite outcome. Then allow several students to explain why they feel their answers are best.

CASE #1

Karen and Jody had been best friends since third grade and were excited to be going to the same junior high school. Although they didn't have many classes together, they made a point to be with each other at breaks and lunch. Karen made friends with a lot of the popular kids because they all had English during the same period. It wasn't long before Karen stopped meeting Jody for lunch, and then she began to forget outings they'd planned. Then Karen started dating Bob, the captain of the baseball team. Bob didn't like Jody and told Karen not to hang around with her anymore.

What should Karen do?

(a) Karen should do what Bob says. After all, it's about time for her to make some new friends.

(b) Karen should realize that Bob isn't her real friend if he tries to run her life. She should break up with him and spend more time with Jody.

(c) Karen should start all over and make a whole new set of friends for her junior high years.

CASE #2

John is in eighth grade but most of his friends are in high school. His friends are planning to spend the night in an old, abandoned building on the outskirts of the city, and they've invited him to go. John knows that his parents are too strict to let him go, but it sounds like fun. His friends say that if he doesn't go it will prove he's chicken.

What should John do?

(a) John should say he can't go because his parents wouldn't approve.

(b) John should tell his parents he's going to spend the night with some friends. He wouldn't be lying, because that's what he's doing. Then his parents would be happy and so would he.

(c) John should sneak out to meet the guys after his parents go to bed and sneak back before his parents wake up.

CASE #3

You're running for class president against Joe. As of the last poll, you're behind by a large percentage. You know you'd make a better president because you want to improve your school. Joe only wants to win to become more popular than he already is. You know Joe has cheated on several exams because you sit next to him in math. He writes all the answers on the bottom of his shoe and looks at it throughout the test.

What should you do?

(a) Tell the math teacher about Joe's cheating.

(b) Begin telling all the students about the cheating and make up a few other things as well. After all, they deserve to know. And you'd be doing them a favor to not have him as a president.

(c) Do nothing and wait for election day.

After the "trials" are over, ask:

● **How was being on a jury and making decisions for these relationships like real life?** (It's sometimes hard to know what is best; making the right decision can be hard.)

Say: **We've looked at some problems that can arise in different kinds of relationships. Today we'll find ways to make our relationships the best.**

Table Talk Follow-Up

If you sent the "Table Talk" handout (p. 19) to parents last week, discuss students' reactions to the activity. Ask volunteers to share what they learned from the discussion with their parents.

I CAN'T HEAR YOU

Have each person find a partner and instruct pairs to sit in chairs on opposite sides of the room, getting as far apart as possible.

Tell all those sitting on one side of the room to look up Ephesians 4:29. Give those on the other side of the room paper and pencils.

Say: **People who have the Bibles must communicate a verse to their partners, who in turn will write it down on the sheet of paper. The only catch is that you have to read the verse backward. The first pair to correctly write the entire verse with the words in the correct order wins.**

Just before you start, play extremely loud music on the radio and say "go!" Be sure the music is loud enough to hinder communication. When someone has the correct verse or two minutes have passed, ask:

● **How did you feel trying to communicate the verse?** (Frustrated; hopeless; angry.)

● **What did it feel like trying to receive the message from your partner?** (Confusing; ridiculous; I couldn't understand.)

● **What would have made communication easier?** (Being closer together; not having loud music; being able to read the words in order.)

● **How is this game like communicating with your friends in real life?** (Sometimes there are distractions keeping us from understanding the other person; if we grow far apart it's not easy to share things.)

Say: **Every relationship has distractions and difficult situations to overcome. Good communication is one way to keep a friendship strong. Let's look at some things God wants us to do to build the best relationships.**

MISSION IMPOSSIBLE

Photocopy the "Mission Impossible" handout (p. 28), cut out the "one another" statements and hide all the messages in the room. Hide only one each of the Positive One Another slips and lots of the Negative One Anothers.

Read the following directions to the students while doing your best spy impersonation. (Wear an overcoat and hat for added effect.)

Say: **Congratulations! You've all been chosen to participate in an important and risky mission. Be careful. Here are your secret instructions: Through our informant we've learned there are 10 excellent relationship qualities out there somewhere, and we want them. If they get into the wrong hands, this mission could be a disaster. We must find them. The risk is we've also discovered there are many counterfeit qualities out there, so don't be fooled. These counterfeits must be found and destroyed. Therefore, for every counterfeit you turn in, you'll receive**

100 points, and for every true characteristic, the reward is 1,500 points. You have three minutes. Good Luck!

Have the students scour the area for the true and counterfeit qualities. When they're finished, have those who think they've found a true relationship quality come to the front and instruct the others to tally their points. Congratulate the winner, naming him or her Top Spy.

Have each person who found a true quality write it on the chalkboard. If kids don't find all 10, add the missing ones by checking the list on page 28. When all 10 have been listed, ask:

● **How do you know these are the characteristics of a true friend, compared to the counterfeit qualities?** (They're positive things; they're things a friend should do.)

● **How was this hunt like relationships you've had?** (Good qualities are harder to find; there are a lot of false friends out there.)

● **Why wouldn't a true friend do the things on the counterfeit slips?** (They're things that destroy friendships; it would be mean.)

● **How do you feel when someone does the things listed on the board?** (Special; loved; cared for; important.)

Have several students volunteer to read aloud John 13:34-35; Romans 12:14-18; and Ephesians 4:29-32.

After each student reads his or her passage, have the group determine which of the 10 items listed on the chalkboard are mentioned. Put a checkmark beside each phrase every time it's referred to. If new items are mentioned, add these to the list.

When all the verses have been read, ask:

● **What kind of friend does all these things?** (A perfect one; Jesus; a friend who loves you.)

● **Why do you think God has given us so many instructions on how to treat others?** (Because God wants our relationships to be more successful; God knows we need help in friendships; God wants us to lead our friends to him.)

Say: **If you can do the things we've listed on the board, you'll certainly be the best friend anyone can find. It's not easy being a good friend, especially when others don't treat you the same way. But God has given us specific directions for having the best relationships possible.**

IT'S WRITTEN ALL OVER YOUR FACE

Have students form a circle. Give each person a pencil and a strip of masking tape 2 to 3 inches long.

Say: **On this piece of tape I'd like you to secretly write something about the person on your right that makes him or her a good friend. Then, without showing that person the tape, place it on his or her forehead.**

When students have done this, have them walk around the

COMMITMENT
(5 to 10 minutes)

room asking others for one-word clues to reveal their qualities. For example, if a person has "good sense of humor" on his or her forehead, others could give clues such as "laugh," "fun" or "joke."

When kids have figured out their qualities, have them each find a partner with a quality different from their own. Ask them to share one way they can express the other person's quality in their own lives in the next week.

Say: **You all have many qualities to make great relationships already, but there are some areas in which you know you could do better. Recognizing areas for improvement is one step toward building stronger friendships.**

CLOSING
(up to 5 minutes)

☐ OPTION 1: RELATE-O-METER

Place a 10-foot strip of masking tape on the floor. Number the tape from 1 to 10 at 1-foot intervals to create a huge rating scale.

Say: **As I read the following statements, rate your attitudes and actions regarding friendship, thinking about the kind of friend you are now. Then stand at the appropriate place on the tape. One means, "This is never true," and 10 means, "This is always true."**

1. **I'd rather watch television than spend time with friends.**
2. **Friends are handy when you forget to do your homework.**
3. **I spend time with my friends only when they invite me to parties.**
4. **I call my friends only if I need money.**
5. **I'd like to be a better friend, but I'm too shy.**
6. **My friends know I care about them even though I sometimes blow it.**
7. **I try to think about how my actions will make my friends feel.**
8. **I'm usually a good friend, but I know I could improve in a couple of areas.**
9. **I reach out to people who seem lonely and make sure my friends know I care about them.**
10. **I encourage others and show them that I value their friendships.**

Have students each link arms with the person standing next to them and pray together that God will help them to be the best friend possible.

☐ OPTION 2: CENTER OF GOD'S LOVE

Have the class stand in a circle and hold hands.

Say: **Imagine the middle of this circle represents God's love. As you look across the circle, you see your friends through God's love. Try to think how God sees those around you.**

Now have kids turn their backs to the center, remaining in a circle.

Say: **When you turn your back on a friend, you can no longer see that person through God's love. Basically you've turned your back on God's love all together.**

Have the class turn back around.

Say: **We've talked about a lot of qualities that are important to great relationships, but the most important quality is to have God's love for each other. That's what will really make our relationships a success.**

Give the class 30 seconds to silently pray for the person to the right. Then close in prayer.

If You Still Have Time ...

Secret Confessions—Have students each write on a slip of paper a situation where they feel they failed to do their best in a relationship. Randomly read these (without names) and allow the class to suggest ways of handling similar situations better in the future.

Relationship Roadblocks—Using the furniture in the room, have the kids create an obstacle course. Each piece of furniture should be given a name representing an obstacle to good relationships. Have the kids run through the course one at a time. When they reach each obstacle, they have to call out a way to overcome this relationship roadblock.

MISSION IMPOSSIBLE

Photocopy this page and cut apart the slips. You'll need at least 10 each of the Negative One Another slips and only <u>one</u> each of the Positive One Another slips.

Negative One Anothers	**Positive One Anothers**
Be jealous of one another.	Love one another.
Fight with one another.	Be kind to one another.
Gossip about one another.	Forgive one another.
Trick one another.	Pray for one another.
Hate one another.	Treat one another better than yourself.
Lie to one another.	Encourage one another.
Curse one another.	Be devoted to one another.
Reject one another.	Respect one another.
Be mean to one another.	Serve one another.
Steal from one another.	Help one another with problems.

BE TRUE TO YOUR SCHOOL

Before a student receives a high school diploma, he or she will have spent over 15,000 hours at school. Only sleep takes up more of a student's time! Because teenagers spend so much time walking down hallways, rummaging through lockers and sitting in desks, it's important that they feel they're succeeding in school.

Success in the eyes of a junior higher can be defined by being popular, getting good grades or making the team. This lesson will help students look at success the way God sees it. They will explore what "doing your best" in school really means.

To challenge junior highers to make their school lives a reflection of their spiritual lives.

LESSON AIM

Students will
- **assess the demands of being a student,**
- **discover how being a student can be a reflection of a person's spiritual life,**
- **see the importance of being a light for Christ in school and**
- **understand the value God places on students.**

OBJECTIVES

Look up the following scripture. Then read the background paragraphs to see how the passage relates to your junior highers and middle schoolers.

In 2 Timothy 2:1-7, a Christian is compared to a soldier, an athlete and a farmer. The goal of a soldier is to please the officer, an athlete is obedient to rules and the farmer receives a reward for his hard work.

BIBLE BASIS
2 TIMOTHY 2:1-7

Just as the soldier, athlete and farmer are examples to Christians, a student can be an example as well. These verses encourage junior highers to be hard-working, focused on God and committed. This passage helps teenagers see that being a student can be a reflection of a person's spiritual life.

THIS LESSON AT A GLANCE

Section	Minutes	What Students Will Do	Supplies
Opener (Option 1)	5 to 10	**Academic Olympics**—Participate in an academic quiz game.	
(Option 2)		**Three Cheers for Us!**—Create and perform a school cheer.	
Action and Reflection	10 to 15	**The Secret of My Success**—Race through the day of a star student.	"The Secret of My Success" handouts (p. 36), combs, pencils, balls
Bible Application	15 to 20	**Student Sketches**—Play a drawing game.	Paper, scissors, pen, small container, newsprint, markers, easel or tape, Bible
Commitment	5 to 10	**This Little Light of Mine**—Witness the value of small lights in a dark place.	Small birthday candles, matches
Closing (Option 1)	up to 5	**Well-Balanced Diet**—Play a game demonstrating balance.	3×5 cards, marker
(Option 2)		**First-Class**—Receive a reminder of who they are.	First-class stamps

The Lesson

OPENER
(5 to 10 minutes)

☐ OPTION 1: ACADEMIC OLYMPICS

Form four teams and have each one choose a school name (such as Harvard or Yale). Students will remain in their "school" teams for the remainder of the meeting.

Have each team select one member as its representative. Place a chair in the middle of the room and have the teams position themselves around the chair. Teams should be approximately four feet from the chair.

Say: **I'm going to read some questions aloud, and the first representative to run up and tag the chair will be** given the opportunity to answer each question. Only the representative may come forward, and each representative only gets one chance to answer, so be sure your team agrees on an answer before you run for the chair.

Award 200 points for a correct answer by the first representative at the chair. If that answer is incorrect, award 100 points to the next team with the correct answer. Ask as many questions as time allows. The team with the highest score wins.

QUESTIONS:

1. Who was the United States' 106th Supreme Court justice? (Clarence Thomas)

2. Which of the nine planets in our solar system is nearest to the sun? (Mercury)

3. What is 1,760 yards more commonly known as? (one mile)

4. Who wrote the book *Alice's Adventures in Wonderland*? (Lewis Carroll)

5. Who discovered the law of gravitation? (Isaac Newton)

6. What are the two major political parties in the United States? (Democratic and Republican)

7. Which of the 50 U.S. states is the largest? (Alaska)

8. What close-fitting garment was named after a French gymnast? (the leotard, after Julius Leotard)

9. What is a baby kangaroo called? (a joey)

10. In what ocean is Wake Island? (Pacific)

11. The Stanley Cup is awarded in what sport? (hockey)

When the game is over, congratulate the winners. You can award gold, silver and bronze "medals" made from foil if you like.

Ask:

● **What were your feelings while participating in this game? Explain.** (I was nervous because I didn't want to let my team down; I felt great because I knew some of the winning answers.)

● **How is this game like school?** (You win or get good grades if you're the best; people expect you to do better than you think you can.)

● **How is this game different from our relationship with God?** (God loves everyone, even "losers"; we don't have to perform for God.)

Say: **Even if you're a straight-A student, school can be tough. It's easy to feel second best sitting next to "Dexter the human brain." But God looks at us as winners when we do our best, no matter what others say. Let's learn more about doing our best at school.**

☐ OPTION 2: THREE CHEERS FOR US!

Form four teams and have each one choose a school name (such as Harvard or Yale). Students will remain in their "school" teams for the remainder of the meeting.

Give teams each three minutes to create a school cheer. Encourage them to incorporate motions or other choreography into their cheers.

Have each team perform its school cheer and have everyone vote as to which team showed the most school spirit. (Teams cannot vote for themselves.) Announce the winning team and have everyone give them a huge cheer.

Say: **We're all usually proud of our schools, and we enjoy cheering for our teams at sports events. But cheering *about* school is another issue! It can be hard to get excited about homework, lectures or doing 50 chin-ups in PE. You may not always get a big cheer for your efforts, but God wants you to do your best in every area of life, including school!**

ACTION AND REFLECTION
(10 to 15 minutes)

THE SECRET OF MY SUCCESS

Say: **School is more than just sitting in class. With sports, clubs and friends also involved, it seems like a lot is expected of you! Let's see which "school" can juggle all the responsibilities the best.**

Give each team a photocopy of "The Secret of My Success" handout (p. 36), a comb, one pencil and a ball of any kind.

Allow two minutes for the teams to read through the handout and decide who will do each activity. (For smaller groups, kids can double up on activities.)

Begin the activity and have everyone cheer for the team that finishes first. Have kids take turns answering the following questions in their groups. Then, have volunteers share insights with the whole group.

● **How did this activity make you feel? Explain.** (Rushed, like this was a normal day; frustrated because it was too confusing.)

● **How was this game like school?** (There are a lot of things to get involved in; there's pressure to do good in many areas.)

● **What other things are important to your success in school?** Answers will vary.

Say: **School really is a challenge. Yet God wants us to do our best. Let's see why it's important to try our best at school.**

BIBLE APPLICATION
(15 to 20 minutes)

STUDENT SKETCHES

Before the meeting, cut four slips of paper and write one of the following words on each slip: "soldier," "athlete," "farmer" and "student." Fold these in half and place them in a small container.

Place large sheets of newsprint and markers on an easel in the front of the room or tape sheets of newsprint to the front wall. Ask each team to choose one member to be the "artist."

Say: **Each team will have a chance to guess the word**

their "artist" is drawing. **The artist may not use any let-**
ters, numbers or other common symbols to depict the
word. The artist may not give any verbal clues, either. I
will time each team, and the team that guesses its word
the fastest wins.

Have the artist from the first team pick a slip of paper from
the container. When he or she picks up a marker from the
easel, begin timing the team as the artist draws. When the
team correctly guesses the word, have the artist write the
word on the paper.

Then have the next team's artist take his or her turn.
Continue until all four words are guessed.

Ask:

● **What do all these occupations have in common?**
(They're all hard-working; all involve commitment.)

Read 2 Timothy 2:1-7 aloud and say: **Paul gives three**
examples of a Christian: a soldier, an athlete, and a farmer,
and we've added a fourth, a student. In your teams, take
one minute to come up with three qualities that are need-
ed for a person to be a success in the occupation you drew.

When the teams are finished, have them each come up to
the front and write their qualities on their drawing.

Ask:

● **Compare the qualities needed in these occupations—**
in what ways are they alike? (All are committed; they all
take a lot of time.)

● **How is each occupation named in the Bible like a**
Christian? (The soldier wants to please his officer, and we
want to please God; the athlete obeys rules to win, and we
must obey God to succeed; the farmer receives a reward for
his work, and God rewards those who serve him.)

● **How is a student an example of a Christian?** (A student learns at school, and we're always learning about God;
students listen to teachers to learn, and we listen to God to
learn.)

● **How could you reflect your Christian faith in the way**
you act as a student? (I could put all my effort into my
schoolwork so that it's my best; I could be on time and prepared for class; I could tell my friends about Christ.)

Say: **Sometimes we think of being a student as dull and**
as something we just have to do whether we like it or not.
But it can be more exciting when we see it as an opportu-
nity to be an example of what it means to be a Christian!

THIS LITTLE LIGHT OF MINE

Have students stand in a circle. Give everyone a small
birthday candle and then turn out any lights in the room.

Ask:

● **How is this darkened room like your school?** (People
are misled because they can't see the truth; kids are looking
for someone to lead them but can't see the way.)

COMMITMENT
(5 to 10 minutes)

● **Being a student involves a lot of different things— what are ways you can be a light for God in your activities at school?** (Speak kind words; encourage others; reach out to lonely kids.)

Say: **We're going to light one another's candles to brighten this room. As you all light the candles of the people next to you, tell them one way you see them being a light for God.**

Light your candle and use it to light the candle of the student next to you while sharing an affirming statement with that person. Then have that person light the candle of the person next to him or her and share an affirming statement. (If you have a large group, light the candles of the students on either side of you so the flame and affirmation move on both sides of the room.)

When the entire room is lit, say: **A bunch of small lights sure brightens up a dark place. Being a student gives you the potential to be a light for God and brighten your school.**

Have kids blow out their candles. Then turn on the lights.

☐ OPTION 1: WELL-BALANCED DIET

Before the meeting, prepare enough 3×5 cards for everyone in your class by writing one of the following words on each card: "social," "spiritual," "academic" or "extracurricular."

Say: **One problem with doing our best in school is getting off balance. Let's play a game so you'll see what I mean.**

Distribute a card to each person. When you say "go," have kids find people with the other three words on their cards to form a team of four. The first team to find one of each card and sit down wins the round.

Have the kids exchange cards and repeat the game several times. Each time students have to find different people for their team.

Say: **To win the game you have to have a balance in four areas. Two "socials" and two "academics" didn't win. To be the best student, you need to balance all these areas in your life.**

Have students each find a partner and share one area they feel is out of balance in their life. Close by having students pray in their pairs for each other.

☐ OPTION 2: FIRST-CLASS

Obtain first-class stamps from the post office and give one to each person in your class.

Say: **In God's eyes you're first-class. He wants you to do your best yet still loves you when you fail. Put this stamp on your Bible or a school binder to remind you that God**

sees you as a first-class student.

Have kids gather in their "school" teams to pray that they each will live like a first-class Christian in the coming week.

If You Still Have Time . . .

How to Be First-Rate—Ask the class a series of questions of "firsts." For example: Who was the first man on the moon? (Neil Armstrong) U.S. president? (George Washington) female on a U.S. coin? (Susan B. Anthony) female U.S. vice-presidential candidate? (Geraldine Ferraro). Have them come up with others. When kids are finished, have each person say what he or she would like to be remembered for being first-rate in.

Second-Class Citizens—Have students brainstorm ways that they and other people settle for second-best. For example, students may be able to get good grades, but because they don't feel like studying, they settle for lower grades. Or workers may do poor jobs because they think no one cares about their work.

Have students think of practical ways to encourage others to be their best in everything they do.

THE Secret of my SUCCESS

Directions: Select one person to do each activity described below. Everyone must do at least one activity, and someone may need to take two turns. When your leader begins the relay, do the activities, in order, as quickly as possible.

In order to be the best at my school, I get up early each morning and groom myself perfectly.
(#1, comb your hair 20 times)

Then it's off to class where I take great notes all during a very boring lecture.
(#2, write the alphabet legibly on the back of this handout and yawn twice)

I'm running for class president, so there's plenty of campaigning to do.
(#3, recite the Pledge of Allegiance)

Then it's off to sports practice. I'm shooting for the pros someday.
(#4 and #5, toss the ball back and forth 20 times)

Being successful also means getting involved in clubs. I'm in the spirit club, and we meet every day.
(#6, shout, "Go team!" 10 times while jumping up and down)

Finally it's time for homework, the final key to my success.
(#7, write the alphabet backward on the back of this handout)

That's it!

CHOOSING OR LOSING GOD'S VALUES

What influences the values of a teenager the most? According to a recent survey, the top five were friends (87 percent), home (51 percent), school (45 percent), music (41 percent) and television (32 percent). Only 13 percent of the students surveyed said religion influences their values.

With so much influence coming from so many sources, we need to be committed to helping junior highers understand God's desires for their lives. This lesson will show them what God values in a Christian's life.

To help junior highers choose values according to God's Word.

LESSON AIM

Students will
- learn how values affect actions,
- discover the difference between the values of God and the values of the world,
- choose which qualities and values God thinks are important and
- commit to make their lives a reflection of God's values.

OBJECTIVES

Look up the following scripture. Then read the background paragraphs to see how the passage relates to your junior highers and middle schoolers.

BIBLE BASIS
1 SAMUEL 16:1-13

First Samuel 16:1-13 is the story of God choosing a king for Israel.

God sent Samuel to Bethlehem to select a king to replace Saul. Visiting the home of Jesse, Samuel found seven tall, strong and handsome sons. He was convinced that God would choose one of these men. But instead God chose David, the eighth and youngest son who was merely a shepherd. God reminded Samuel that while the world looks at one's appearance, he looks at the heart.

Junior highers live in a world where appearance is of utmost importance. To fit in, they must wear the right clothes, style their hair just so and own a variety of expensive "toys." Self-worth is based on the opinions of others. It's important to help students discover that they're valuable to God no matter how they look or what they own.

THIS LESSON AT A GLANCE

Section	Minutes	What Students Will Do	Supplies
Opener (Option 1)	5 to 10	**Molder of My Heart**—Use clay to create something they value.	Modeling clay
(Option 2)		**Values Brainstorm**—Define values.	Newsprint, marker
Action and Reflection	15 to 20	**Auction, Auction!**—Participate in an auction to purchase "goods."	Various "auctionable" items, play money, bag
Bible Application	10 to 15	**Bag Full of Me**—Decorate masks that reflect how others see them.	Paper grocery bags, markers, Bible
Commitment	5 to 10	**Inside Out**—Show a side of themselves that others don't see.	Markers, bags from "Bag Full of Me" activity
Closing (Option 1)	up to 5	**Reflect on This**—See themselves as a reflection of God's values.	Mirror, box
(Option 2)		**The Hardest Part**—Tell situations where it's hard to have God's values.	

The Lesson

OPENER
(5 to 10 minutes)

☐ OPTION 1: MOLDER OF MY HEART

Give students each a hunk of clay and tell them they have two minutes to mold it into something they value greatly, such as a car, a boyfriend or girlfriend, clothes or money.

When finished, have kids each find a partner and share how having this value has affected their actions. For example, if they value clothes, they may work in order to have more money for their wardrobes.

When everyone has shared, ask:

● **What are ways your values affect your actions?** (Getting a job to make money; taking good care of my body.)

● **How does having that value make you feel?** (I have a goal; something is important about me; loved.)

● **Why do you think valuing something changes our behavior?** (Because it's the most important thing in my life; because I have to work hard to keep it.)

Say: **Everybody values something. Today we're going to talk about the things God values and why these are the best things we can value.**

☐ OPTION 2: VALUES BRAINSTORM

Write the word "values" at the top of a sheet of newsprint.

Say: **Let's take a minute to brainstorm definitions of this word.**

Encourage kids to suggest possible meanings of the word "values." Kids might say things like priorities, honesty or code of conduct. Write kids' ideas on the newsprint.

Afterward, ask:

● **Was it easy for you to define this word? Why or why not?** (Yes, because my family talks about values a lot; no, because I've never really thought about it.)

Say: **Defining values may be easy or difficult, but applying them to our lives is something we all struggle with. Today we're going to look at the best values one can have: God's values.**

AUCTION, AUCTION!

Before the meeting, gather a number of items for an auction. Items should be of varying values and can include a candy bar, a half-off coupon for your next youth event, a pencil, a can of soda, a book or items never claimed from your lost-and-found box.

Put a large amount of play money of various values in a bag and have students reach inside and take two bills. (Slips of paper with numbers written on them can be used as well.)

Say: **We're going to have an auction! You can buy something with the "money" you have or form a pool with others to buy something to share.**

Begin the bidding, keeping a quick pace. After all the items have been purchased, ask:

● **How did you feel during the auction? Explain.** (Frustrated because I wanted something but didn't have enough money; happy because I got what I wanted; angry because no one would pool their money with me.)

● **How is the way we acted during this auction like the way people act when pursuing things they value?** (People are aggressive in going for what they want; some people don't care about material things.)

● **How did our auction reflect our values?** (Money is hard to get, and we only wanted to spend it on important things; we couldn't buy some things, but we still tried to get them.)

● **If you could have bought feelings at this auction, what would you buy?** (Peace of mind; the feeling of being loved; the feeling of being forgiven.)

● **How much would you be willing to pay for these feelings?** (Nothing; half of what I own; everything.)

Say: **Just like this auction, you can tell what people value by what they spend their money on and what they spend their time doing. Hopefully those things are pleasing to God, but what does God really value after all? Let's look at what the Bible says.**

BAG FULL OF ME

Give each student a large paper grocery bag and provide markers to be shared by all.

Say: **Take your bag and determine where holes for eyes should be. Tear these out. Then write words or draw pictures on the outside of your bag expressing characteristics others see when they look at you. For example, you might draw a smile or write the word "happy." These words or drawings don't have to represent how *you* feel about yourself but how you think *others* see you. On the inside of the bag, draw or write things representing what you feel is important about yourself that others may not know.**

When students are finished, have them put their bags over their heads and form groups of no more than four. In their groups, have students look at the outside of one another's bags and determine what the words or drawings represent.

Read 1 Samuel 16:1-13 aloud and have students summarize the story in their own words.

Ask:

● **From these verses, what do you think are things God values?** (How you are on the inside; the things about you others don't always see.)

● **How do you feel when people judge you based on the things on the outside of your bag?** (Nervous that I won't live up to their expectations; unfairly judged; angry.)

● **How are the things that seem important to others different from the things God values?** (We look at popularity or money; God looks at the heart as the most important thing, but we look at appearances.)

Say: **As you all wear your bags, you look a lot alike. It's what's on the inside that makes each of you very special. It's nice to know that God values what's on the inside of** us rather than on the outside. But let's make sure what's on the inside is pleasing to him. We want to be our best on the inside, too.

INSIDE OUT

Have students remain in their groups and take off their paper bags. Have markers available.

Say: **Turn your bags inside out and look at the words or pictures on your bag. See if any of them represent values not pleasing to God or just things you'd like to change. Draw a line through any of these things and pray as a group for God to bring about change in these areas.**

When students have prayed, ask them to put their bags back on their heads, inside out.

Say: **While wearing your bags with your "real" side showing, write on the bags of your group members the things you think God values in their lives. For example, you might write that God values their commitment to the youth group or their kindness to others.**

When everyone has done this, gather the group together and let kids remove their bags again.

Say: **We can make ourselves more beautiful on the inside by choosing values pleasing to God. No matter what others see on the outside, God is still looking at the part of you that matters most: the inside.**

☐ OPTION 1: REFLECT ON THIS

Before the meeting, place a large mirror in the bottom of a box with a lid.

Pass the box around the class and ask everyone to secretly look inside the box to see something that is a reflection of God. After everyone has looked inside the box, ask:

● **How can our lives reflect God's values?** (We can be an example to others; the way we act shows what we value.)

Say: **God cares about what's in our hearts and thinks those things are most valuable. Let's commit to reflecting God's values by remembering to look at others' hearts, not just their outward appearances.**

Close in prayer, thanking God for showing us the most important things in life.

☐ OPTION 2: THE HARDEST PART

In groups of no more than four, have each person finish the following sentence: "It's hard to have God's values when . . ." For example, "It's hard to have God's values when my friends make fun of people I know God wants me to love." Then have the groups close by praying for strength in these situations.

COMMITMENT
(5 to 10 minutes)

CLOSING
(up to 5 minutes)

If You Still Have Time . . .

One Man's Trash—Have students discuss the saying, "One man's trash is another man's treasure." Have them think of items others value that they find worthless, such as Lawrence Welk albums, abstract art or a food processor.

Course Reflection—Form a circle. Ask students to reflect on the past four lessons. Have them take turns completing the following sentences:

● Something I learned in this course is . . .

● If I could tell my friends about this course, I'd say . . .

● Something I'll do differently because of this course is . . .

BONUS IDEAS

Photo Safari— Have students participate in a Polaroid car rally looking for things illustrating the idea of "best" or "first." Form teams of no more than five. Each team will need a Polaroid camera, film and transportation. Provide a list of local spots or items that students can photograph, such as a "Quality" Inn motel, a blue ribbon or a trophy, a "First" National Bank or a "First" Baptist Church sign. Allot 100 points for each item on the list and explain that you'll award extra points for more creative pictures that students take.

Specify a return time and place. Give each team a sheet of posterboard on which to mount all their pictures and give awards to the winning team.

Bonus Scriptures— The lessons focus on a select few scripture passages, but if you'd like to incorporate more Bible readings into the lessons, here are our suggestions:

● 1 Samuel 15:20-22 (God wants our obedience, not our sacrifice.)

● 2 Samuel 24:22-25 (We need to give our best to God, not freebies and leftovers.)

● 2 Chronicles 16:9 (God supports those who look completely to him.)

● Romans 12:1-2 (God wants us to please *him,* not those of the world.)

● Philippians 3:12-14 (Constantly strive for the best.)

● Hebrews 12:1-3 (Focus on Jesus to be your best.)

Becoming My Best— Have an evening of opportunities to become better at something. For instance, have someone who is good on in-line skates lead a class on skating basics. Have a cooking, shirt painting or sewing class. Have volleyball players from the high school team give pointers and tips. Be creative and offer a wide selection.

People Scavenger Hunt— Before your meeting, secretly contact students' parents to find an area in which each one has excelled. It could be winning a spelling bee in second grade, participating in a beauty pageant at age 3 or something more recent. Print all the information in the style of a Bingo card and hand them out at the meeting. Students must find the people who accomplished each activity and get their signatures. Award prizes for five signatures in a row or for a complete "blackout."

MEETINGS AND MORE

Who Am I?— Before the meeting, write the names of famous achievers on pieces of paper. Include current sports heroes, world leaders, popular entertainers, famous scientists and artists. As students enter for the meeting, tape one of the pieces to each person's back. Have students walk around asking yes-and-no questions to figure out who the individuals are and what they achieved. When students each know their character, discuss what qualities made these people "excellent."

My Heart: Christ's Home— Obtain copies of the booklet "My Heart: Christ's Home" (InterVarsity) from your local Christian bookstore. Hand it out the week prior to the meeting and ask students to read it. At the meeting, discuss the meaning of the booklet, and why it's important to give God the best of everything we do and not just the leftovers.

Table Talk— Use the "Table Talk" handout (p. 19) as the basis for a meeting with parents and teenagers. During the meeting, have parents and kids complete the handout and discuss it.

Have parents and kids form groups of no more than six. Ask each group to share a way they try to do their best each day. Have each group choose one of these ways and create a skit to perform for the other groups. After all groups have participated, ask:

- **In what areas is it important to do your best?**
- **Is there any area where doing your best doesn't matter?**
- **How can we lovingly encourage others to do their best?**

Have everyone remain in their groups and ask each person to share an area in which doing their best is a big struggle. Have group members pray for one another.

Giving My Best Away— Have students plan a day of community service as a way of giving their best to those in need. Help your group choose an activity that is needed in your community and is interesting to them. For example, deliver meals to shut-in elderly people, put on a variety show in a hospital's children's ward or provide an afternoon of games, crafts, music and refreshments in a needy section of town.

PARTY PLEASER

My Hero— Have a costume party where kids come dressed up as people who excelled in what they did, were the best or were great leaders. Take the group bowling or mini-golfing and have contests in categories such as best encourager, best score, most creative stroke (or throw) and best costume. End the evening with "first-class floats" made with soft drinks and ice cream.

Junior High Olympics— Plan a retreat based on the Olympics. Begin by forming teams. Have each team create a country to represent (such as "Superbia" or "Championland"), make a national flag and come up with a national anthem.

Have teams compete in a variety of areas, such as cabin appearance, team spirit and sports events. Make sure to have an opening and closing ceremony, complete with gold, silver and bronze medals at the end while the winning teams sing their national anthems.

Meetings can be centered around living lives of Olympic quality for God. Talk about what it takes to be a gold-medal Christian.

RETREAT IDEA

Capture Your Teenagers' Attention With Boredom-Busting, Topical, 4-week Studies for Junior and Senior High Students

FOR JUNIOR HIGH/MIDDLE SCHOOL:

Accepting Others: Beyond Barriers & Stereotypes	1-55945-126-2
Advice to Young Christians: Exploring Paul's Letters	1-55945-146-7
Applying the Bible to Life	1-55945-116-5
Becoming Responsible	1-55945-109-2
Bible Heroes: Joseph, Esther, Mary & Peter	1-55945-137-8
Boosting Self-Esteem	1-55945-100-9
Building Better Friendships	1-55945-138-6
Can Christians Have Fun?	1-55945-134-3
Christmas: A Fresh Look	1-55945-124-6
Doing Your Best	1-55945-142-4
Guys & Girls: Understanding Each Other	1-55945-110-6
Handling Conflict	1-55945-125-4
Heaven & Hell	1-55945-131-9
Is God Unfair?	1-55945-108-4
Making Parents Proud	1-55945-107-6
The Miracle of Easter	1-55945-143-2
Miracles!	1-55945-117-3
Peer Pressure	1-55945-103-3
Prayer	1-55945-104-1
Sermon on the Mount	1-55945-129-7
Telling Your Friends About Christ	1-55945-114-9
The Ten Commandments	1-55945-127-0
Today's Media: Choosing Wisely	1-55945-144-0
Today's Music: Good or Bad?	1-55945-101-7
What Is God's Purpose for Me?	1-55945-132-7
What's a Christian?	1-55945-105-X

FOR SENIOR HIGH:

Angels, Demons, Miracles & Prayer	1-55945-235-8
Christians in a Non-Christian World	1-55945-224-2
Communicating With Friends	1-55945-228-5
Dating Decisions	1-55945-215-3
Dealing With Life's Pressures	1-55945-232-3
Exploring Ethical Issues	1-55945-225-0
Faith for Tough Times	1-55945-216-1
Getting Along With Parents	1-55945-202-1
Getting Along With Your Family	1-55945-233-1
The Gospel of John: Jesus' Teachings	1-55945-208-0
Hazardous to Your Health: AIDS, Steroids & Eating Disorders	1-55945-200-5
Is Marriage in Your Future?	1-55945-203-X
The Joy of Serving	1-55945-210-2
Knowing God's Will	1-55945-205-6
Making Good Decisions	1-55945-209-9
Movies, Music, TV & Me	1-55945-213-7
Psalms	1-55945-234-X
Real People, Real Faith	1-55945-238-2
Revelation	1-55945-229-3
School Struggles	1-55945-201-3
Sex: A Christian Perspective	1-55945-206-4
Who Is God?	1-55945-218-8
Who Is Jesus?	1-55945-219-6
Who Is the Holy Spirit?	1-55945-217-X
Your Life as a Disciple	1-55945-204-8

MORE INNOVATIVE RESOURCES FOR YOUR YOUTH MINISTRY

The Youth Worker's Encyclopedia of Bible-Teaching Ideas: Old Testament/ New Testament

Explore the most comprehensive idea-books available for youth workers! Discover more than 360 creative ideas in each of these 416-page encyclopedias—there's at least one idea for each and every book of the Bible. Find ideas for...retreats and overnighters, learning games, adventures, special projects, parties, prayers, music, devotions, skits, and much more!

Plus, you can use these ideas for groups of all sizes in any setting. Large or small. Sunday or mid-week meeting. Bible study. Sunday school class or retreat. Discover exciting new ways to teach each book of the Bible to your youth group.

Old Testament   ISBN 1-55945-184-X
New Testament   ISBN 1-55945-183-1

Clip-Art Cartoons for Churches

Here are over 180 funny, photocopiable illustrations to help you jazz up your calendars, newsletters, posters, fliers, transparencies, postcards, business cards, announcements—all your printed materials! These fun, fresh illustrations cover a variety of church and Christian themes, including church life, Sunday school, youth groups, school life, sermons, church events, volunteers, and more! And there's a variety of artistic styles to choose from so each piece you create will be unique and original.

Each illustration is provided in the sizes you need most, so it's easy to use. You won't find random images here...each image is a complete cartoon. And these cartoons are fun! In fact, they're so entertaining that you may just find yourself reading the book and not photocopying them at all.

Order your copy of **Clip-Art Cartoons for Churches** today...and add some spice to your next printed piece.

ISBN 1-55945-791-0

Bore No More! (For Every Pastor, Speaker, Teacher)

This book is a must for every pastor, youth leader, teacher, and speaker. These 70 audience-grabbing activities pull listeners into your lesson or sermon—and drive your message home!

Discover clever object lessons, creative skits, and readings. Music and celebration ideas. Affirmation activities. All the innovative techniques 85 percent of adult churchgoers say they wish their pastors would try! (recent Group Publishing poll)

Involve your congregation in the learning process! These complete 5- to 15-minute activities highlight common New Testament Lectionary passages, so you'll use this book week after week.

ISBN 1-55945-266-8

Order today from your local Christian bookstore, or write:
Group Publishing, Box 485, Loveland, CO 80539.